ANN MORRIS

ON THE GO

PHOTOGRAPHS BY KEN HEYMAN

HOUGHTON MIFFLIN COMPANY

BOSTON

ATLANTA   DALLAS   GENEVA, ILLINOIS   PALO ALTO   PRINCETON

Photograph at bottom of page 16 courtesy of Jayce Fox.
Photographs pages 27-29 courtesy of NASA.

On the Go, by Ann Morris, photographs by Ken Heyman. Text copyright © 1990 by Ann Morris.
Photographs copyright © 1990 by Ken Heyman. Reprinted by permission of Lothrop, Lee &
Shepard Books, a division of William Morrow & Company, Inc.

Houghton Mifflin Edition, 1996
Copyright © 1996 by Houghton Mifflin Company. All rights reserved.

Printed in the U.S.A.

ISBN: 0-395-75332-5

123456789-B-99 98 97 96 95

All over the world
people move from place to place
carrying babies on their backs,

5

6   baskets over their shoulders,

and almost anything on their heads.

7

They travel on foot.
They ride on horses and donkeys

and camels.

Wheels make things go easier and faster.

They can be pedaled
or pushed...

11

or pulled by ponies

or oxen...

14   or people.

Some wheels are powered by motors.

15

A fire engine hurries
to put out the fire.

Buses carry people all over town.

18   All aboard! Trains switch from track to track.

A trolley moves on rails along the city street.

Zoom!
You can go
150 miles an hour
on a monorail.

People travel on water, too.
Some row their boats.

Others push them along with poles.

Some people sell refreshments from their boats. 21

22   Sailors hope for a good wind.

Tugboats guide ships
from all over
the world
into the harbor.

23

Jet planes carry people and cargo across continents.

You can go straight up in a helicopter

or a rocket....Liftoff! 27

Maybe one day
you will travel to the moon.

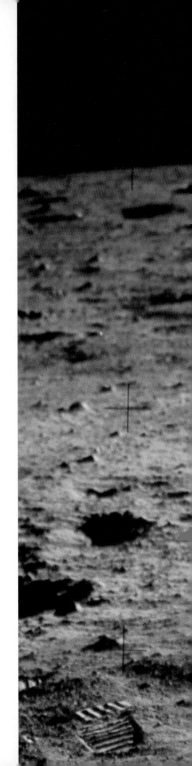